WHERE I LIVE

By the Seaside

Honor Head

WAYLAND

Explore the world with **Popcorn** - your complete first non-fiction library.

Look out for more titles in the Popcorn range. All books have the same format of simple text and striking images. Text is carefully matched to the pictures to help readers to identify and understand key vocabulary.
www.waylandbooks.co.uk/popcorn

First published in 2010 by Wayland
Copyright © Wayland 2010

Wayland
Hachette Children's Books
338 Euston Road
London NW1 3BH

Wayland Australia
Level 17/207 Kent Street
Sydney NSW 2000

Produced for Wayland by
White-Thomson Publishing Ltd
www.wtpub.co.uk
+44 (0)843 208 7460

Editor: Jean Coppendale
Designer: Amy Sparks
Commissioned photography: Chris Fairclough
Picture Researcher: Amy Sparks
Series consultant: Kate Ruttle
Design concept: Paul Cherrill

The author and publisher would like to thank Alex, Alicia,
Katherine and their parents for all their help with this book.
With special thanks to Seasports, Teignmouth, Devon.

British Library Cataloging in Publication Data
Honor Head
By The Seaside - (Popcorn. Where I Live)
1. Seaside resorts -- Great Britain -- Pictorial works -- Juvenile literature
2. Coasts--Great Britain--Pictorial works--Juvenile literature.
I. Title II. Series
941.009746-dc22

ISBN: 978 0 7502 6315 3

Wayland is a division of Hachette Children's Books,
an Hachette UK company.
www.hachette.co.uk

Printed and bound in China

Contents

The seaside 4

My school 6

After school 8

On the seafront 10

On the beach 12

At the weekend 14

Summer jobs 16

Shopping 18

Getting about 20

Who works at the seaside? 22

Glossary 24

Index 24

The seaside

My name is Alex. I live at the seaside.
I can see the sea from my window.

My house is one
of a row of
terraced houses.

Near my house there is a harbour where people keep their boats. My mum and dad own a sailing boat. We often go sailing at the weekends for fun.

The boats are used for fishing, sailing and rowing.

fishing boat

sailing boat

rowing boat

motor boat

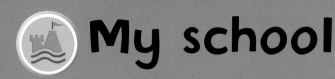 My school

My school is a short walk from my house.
Each day two of the parents take a group
of us to school and bring us home.

The parents make sure we get
to school and home safely.

Sometimes our teacher takes
us to the beach to look at rock
pools. These are pools of seawater
trapped by the rocks.

We look for sea animals such as crabs and starfish.

After school

After school we like to go swimming in the sea if the water is not too rough. We always swim where the safety flags and lifeguards are.

The lifeguards make sure swimmers are safe in the sea.

The lifeguards are all volunteers which means they do the work for free.

RNLI LIFEGUARD

Sometimes we watch the life boat crew practising in their special boat. The crew rescue boats and people that need help far out at sea.

The life boat crews save many lives every year.

On the seafront

People walk along the seafront by the beach to enjoy the fresh sea air. When the weather is bad the waves come up over the seafront.

Some people like to sit and enjoy the scenery.

The pier has lots
of things for people
to do when it is
too cold to sit
on the beach.

On the pier are
childrens' rides
and a shop to
buy popcorn.

A pier is a long
platform that
stretches from
the seafront into
the sea.

On the beach

I like to play on the beach with my cousins. We build sandcastles and collect shells. During the summer there are sandcastle building competitions on the beach.

What would you like to do on the beach?

12

The beach where I live is made of rough sand. Some beaches are made of pebbles or stones.

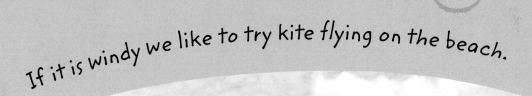

If it is windy we like to try kite flying on the beach.

At the weekend

My mum and dad run a sea sports centre so they have to work at the weekend. Sometimes I go to the centre with them.

At the sea sports centre you can hire canoes and sail boats.

canoe

14

My cousins are learning how to sail a boat. They wear wetsuits, a life jacket and safety helmets to make sure they stay safe in the water.

life jacket

wetsuit

safety helmet

Summer jobs

Some people like to go to the seaside
to work during the summer holidays.

People can work part-time as waiters or
waitresses serving in cafes and restaurants.

This student is working during her summer holidays. She picks up litter on the seafront.

LITTER ONLY

She wears gloves to stop her hands getting dirty.

Shopping

There are lots of shops selling toys for the beach such as buckets and spades and beach balls. The shopkeeper puts lots of his goods on show outside the shop.

What would you like to buy from this shop?

We do not have a big shopping
centre where I live or any big stores.
This is my local newsagent where
we buy magazines and newspapers.

postcards

This shop sells postcards so people can write
to tell their friends about their holiday.

Getting around

We catch a bus to go to the nearest
big town to shop at the chain stores.
There is also a hospital and a cinema
in the nearby town.

We pay the driver when we get on the bus.

Sometimes we take the train to visit my aunty who lives nearby. Many people take the train to work each day.

Trains travel across the country carrying passengers from one place to another.

Taking a train or bus to work each day is called commuting.

Who works at the seaside?

Can you remember what jobs people do at the seaside? Match the pictures opposite to the jobs below to find out.

1. Keeping the seafront clean.

2. Making sure swimmers are safe.

3. Working in a restaurant or café.

4. Hiring out sea sports equipment.

5. Rescuing boats in trouble at sea.

a

Glossary

chain stores   shops owned by the same company that have the same name and sell the same things

goods   items that a shop sells

harbour   a place where ships and boats stay when they are not being used

part-time   when someone works for only part of the day or only a few days a week not the whole working week

terrace   a group of houses joined together on either side

wetsuit   a special suit that you wear in the water if it is cold to keep you warm

Index

beach 7, 10, 11, 12, 13, 19
boats 5
bucket and spade 18

canoes 14
commuting 21

harbour 5

life boats 9
lifeguards 8

pier 11
popcorn 11
postcards 19

rock pools 7

sailing 5
sailing boats 5, 14
safety flags 8
sand 13
sandcastles 12

scenery 10
sea 4
seafront 10, 17
sea sports 14
shells 12
summer holidays 16
swimming 8

waves 10

Where I Live

Contents of titles in the series:

City 978 07502 6318 4

The city
My school
After school
The high street
Getting around
Commuting
Tourists
The River Thames
Shopping
A day in the city
Glossary
Index

Island 978 07502 6317 7

Our island
Rocks and beaches
The village
My school
Boats and planes
Summer visitors
Wildlife
Jobs
Having fun
Island quiz
Glossary
Index

Seaside 978 07502 6315 3

The seaside
My school
After school
On the seafront
On the beach
At the weekend
Summer jobs
Shopping
Getting about
Who works at the seaside?
Glossary
Index

Village 978 07502 6316 0

My village
My school
After school
Village church
At the weekend
At the farm
Shopping
Village shops
Getting around
Who works where?
Glossary
Index

WAYLAND